Raising Grateful

in an Entitled World

*Parents' Guide to Nurturing Gratitude and Humility
in Kids in a Seemingly Entitled World*

Watson R. Ward

Copyright ©
Watson R. Ward

© 2024 USA

All rights reserved. No part of this book may be reproduced or modified in any form, including photocopying, recording, or by any information storage and retrieval system, without permission in writing from the publisher.

Gratitude

Thank you from the bottom of my heart for purchasing this book. Your support means more than words can express.

In choosing to invest your time and energy into nurturing gratitude and humility in your children, you're making a profound impact—not just on their lives, but on the world around them.

Writing this book has been a labor of love, inspired by the everyday heroes like you who strive to raise kind, empathetic, and grounded kids in an often overwhelming and fast-paced world.

Your dedication to fostering these values is incredibly inspiring, and it's my hope that the insights and strategies shared within these pages resonate with you and provide practical, heartfelt guidance on this important journey.

Every page is written with the belief that together, we can cultivate a more grateful and humble generation, one small step at a time.

Thank you for being a part of this mission and for your commitment to making a positive difference in your child's life.

Table of Contents

Copyright © 2

Gratitude 3

Table of Contents 5

Introduction 7

Understanding Entitlement Culture 10

The Impact of Entitlement on Children's Behavior and Attitudes 15

The Importance of Gratitude in Child Development 20

Practical Strategies to Teach Children Gratitude 25

Encouraging a Thankful Mindset in Daily Life 30

Fostering Humility 35

Ways to Nurture Humility in Children 40

Teaching Children the Value of Empathy and Perspective-Taking 44

Strategies for Teaching Empathy and Perspective Taking 46

Setting Boundaries and Limits 51

Teaching Children the Concept of Delayed Gratification 57

Balancing Discipline and Positive Reinforcement 61

Modeling Gratefulness and Humility 66

Practicing Gratitude and Humility in Everyday Interactions . 72

Overcoming Challenges and Building Resilience 77

Strategies for Navigating Peer Pressure and Societal Influences 82

Building Resilience in Children to Combat Entitlement Tendencies 88

Encouraging Ongoing Reflection and Growth in Parenting .. 93

Emphasizing the Long-Term Benefits of Raising Grateful and Humble Children 97

Navigating Disappointments and Setbacks 101

Teaching the Value of Hard Work and Patience 106

Addressing Peer Pressure and Comparisons 113

Coping with Materialism in a Consumer-Driven World 119

Helping Kids Navigate Social and Academic Pressures 127

Conclusion 134

Introduction

Welcome! If you're reading this, chances are you're a parent, grandparent, or caregiver who's noticed how quickly the world around us seems to be changing.

Maybe you've felt a twinge of concern seeing how easily our kids can get caught up in a culture of instant gratification and entitlement.

If so, you're not alone. In a world where the latest gadgets, likes on social media, and immediate rewards often take center stage, nurturing gratitude and humility in our children can feel like an uphill battle.

But here's the good news: you're not in this alone, and it's definitely not a lost cause. This book is your companion on a journey toward raising kids who are grounded, grateful, and humble.

Together, we'll explore practical tips, share heartfelt stories, and uncover the small yet powerful ways you can make a big difference in your child's life.

Think of this book as a conversation between friends.

We'll chat about the joys and challenges of parenting in today's fast-paced world and discover strategies to help our kids appreciate what they have, recognize the efforts of others, and develop a deep sense of empathy and humility.

Throughout these pages, you'll find encouragement, practical advice, and a lot of understanding. Parenting is a tough job, but it's also incredibly rewarding.

By focusing on gratitude and humility, we're not just helping our children—we're also making our homes, communities, and the world a kinder, more compassionate place.

So, grab a cup of coffee or tea, find a cozy spot, and let's dive in. Here's to raising the next generation of grateful, humble, and wonderful human beings, one small step at a time.

Understanding Entitlement Culture

Definition of Entitlement in Children

Entitlement in children refers to a belief or attitude characterized by an exaggerated sense of deservingness, self-importance, and expectation of special treatment or privileges without necessarily putting in the effort or demonstrating the corresponding behavior to earn such rewards.

Children who exhibit entitlement behavior often feel that they are owed certain things or opportunities simply because of who they are, rather than through their own hard work, merit, or contribution.

This sense of entitlement can manifest in various ways, such as:

1. Expecting Rewards Without Effort: Children with a sense of entitlement may believe that they deserve rewards, praise, or material possessions without having to work for them.

They may feel entitled to high grades, special privileges, or expensive gifts without putting in the necessary effort or showing appreciation for what they receive.

2. Lack of Gratitude:

Entitled children may struggle to express genuine gratitude or appreciation for the things they are given. They might take things for granted and fail to recognize the efforts or sacrifices made by others to provide for them.

3. Demanding Behavior:

Children with a sense of entitlement may exhibit demanding behavior, expecting to have their needs met immediately and without question.

They might become upset or throw tantrums when they don't get their way, displaying a lack of patience or understanding of others' perspectives.

4. Difficulty Handling Failure or Disappointment:

Entitled children may struggle to cope with failure, setbacks, or disappointments, as they are accustomed to getting what they want without facing challenges. They may exhibit a sense of entitlement to success and become frustrated or disillusioned when things do not go their way.

5. Lack of Empathy:

Children who feel entitled may have difficulty empathizing with others or understanding different perspectives.

Their focus on their own needs and desires can lead to a lack of consideration for how their actions or words impact those around them.

Recognizing and addressing entitlement in children is important for fostering humility, gratitude, and a strong work ethic.

Parents and caregivers can help children develop a healthy sense of self-worth and appreciation for others by encouraging empathy, resilience, and a willingness to work hard for their goals.

The Impact of Entitlement on Children's Behavior and Attitudes

Entitlement can have significant negative effects on children's behavior and attitudes, shaping their worldview and interactions with others.

The following are some of the major impact of entitlement on children's behavior and attitudes:

1. Lack of Appreciation:

Entitled children often struggle to appreciate the value of what they have, leading to a sense of entitlement towards material possessions, privileges, and opportunities. This lack of appreciation can manifest in ungrateful behavior, where children take things for granted without understanding the effort or resources involved in providing for them.

2. Sense of Entitlement:

Children who grow up feeling entitled may develop a skewed perspective on their rights and responsibilities.

They may expect special treatment or advantages without demonstrating the corresponding effort or gratitude.

This sense of entitlement can hinder their ability to empathize with others and understand the concept of earning rewards through hard work.

3. Lack of Resilience:

Entitled children may struggle with setbacks and challenges, as they are accustomed to having their desires met without facing significant obstacles.

This lack of resilience can lead to frustration, anger, and a sense of helplessness when things do not go their way.

Over time, these children may develop a fear of failure and an aversion to taking risks.

4. Diminished Empathy:

Entitlement can erode children's capacity for empathy and compassion towards others. When children are focused on their own desires and needs, they may struggle to recognize and respond to the feelings and needs of those around them. This lack of empathy can hinder the development of healthy relationships and social skills.

5. Unrealistic Expectations:

Entitled children may harbor unrealistic expectations about life, believing that they are entitled to constant success, praise, and recognition.

When these expectations are not met, children may experience feelings of disappointment, inadequacy, and resentment.

This cycle of unrealistic expectations can perpetuate a sense of entitlement and hinder personal growth and self-improvement.

By addressing the impact of entitlement on children's behavior and attitudes, parents and caregivers can cultivate a sense of gratitude, humility, and resilience in their children.

Through intentional parenting strategies and modeling positive behavior, children can learn to appreciate the value of hard work, empathy, and humility in navigating the complexities of the world around them.

The Importance of Gratitude in Child Development

Gratitude is a powerful virtue that plays a crucial role in shaping a child's development.

In today's fast-paced and materialistic world, instilling a sense of gratitude in children is more important than ever.

The following are the significance of gratitude in nurturing well-rounded and emotionally intelligent children.

Building Empathy and Compassion
Gratitude serves as a cornerstone for developing empathy and compassion in children. When children learn to appreciate the kindness and generosity of others, they

are more likely to empathize with the feelings and experiences of those around them. By acknowledging and being grateful for the efforts of others, children learn to understand the value of kindness and compassion.

Fostering Positive Relationships Gratitude is essential for building and maintaining positive relationships with family, friends, and the community.

Children who express gratitude are more likely to have strong interpersonal skills, as they are able to recognize and acknowledge the contributions and support of others.

Grateful children are also more likely to form meaningful connections based on mutual respect and appreciation.

Cultivating Resilience and Optimism
Practicing gratitude helps children develop a positive outlook on life, even in the face of challenges and setbacks.

When children focus on what they are thankful for, they are better equipped to cope with adversity and setbacks.

Gratitude encourages a mindset of resilience and optimism, teaching children to find silver linings and opportunities for growth in difficult situations.

Promoting Emotional Well-being
Gratitude is closely linked to emotional well-being and mental health. Children who cultivate a sense of gratitude experience higher levels of happiness, satisfaction, and overall well-being. By recognizing and

expressing gratitude for the positive aspects of their lives, children develop a sense of contentment and fulfillment that contributes to their emotional resilience and mental health.

Instilling Values and Virtues
Gratitude is not just a feeling but a value that underpins a range of positive virtues such as humility, generosity, and patience.

When children learn to be grateful, they also develop a sense of humility by acknowledging their own blessings and privileges. Gratitude encourages children to be generous and giving, as they understand the joy of sharing with others.

In conclusion, the importance of gratitude in child development cannot be overstated. By fostering gratitude in children, parents and caregivers lay the foundation for a lifetime of emotional intelligence, resilience, and positive relationships.

Practical Strategies to Teach Children Gratitude

Express Gratitude Daily

Encourage children to express gratitude every day by starting a gratitude journal or incorporating a gratitude practice into their daily routine.

Encourage them to write down or share at least three things they are grateful for each day.

Lead by Example

Children learn best by observing the behavior of adults around them. Model gratitude by expressing your own appreciation for things, people, and experiences in your life. Show them how to say thank you and demonstrate genuine appreciation.

Practice Mindfulness

Teach children to be present in the moment and appreciate the little things in life. Encourage them to notice the beauty around them, such as nature, acts of kindness, or moments of joy.

Mindfulness can help children cultivate a sense of gratitude for the present moment.

Volunteer and Give Back

Engage children in acts of service and volunteering to help them understand the importance of giving back to others. Whether it's volunteering at a local charity, helping a neighbor, or donating toys to a shelter, children can learn empathy and gratitude by helping those in need.

Encourage Perspective Taking

Help children see things from different perspectives by discussing how others may have different experiences or challenges. This can help children develop empathy and a greater appreciation for their own blessings.

Create Gratitude Rituals

Establish family rituals that promote gratitude, such as a gratitude jar where family members can write down moments of appreciation and read them together at the end of each week. These rituals can help reinforce the practice of gratitude in daily life.

Encourage Thank You Notes

Teach children the importance of expressing gratitude through handwritten thank you notes.

Encourage them to write thank you notes for gifts, acts of kindness, or gestures of help they receive. This practice can help children understand the impact of expressing gratitude.

Foster a Gratitude Mindset

Encourage children to shift their focus from what they lack to what they have. Help them see the positive aspects of their lives and cultivate a mindset of abundance and gratitude.

Encourage them to reflect on their blessings and appreciate the good things in their lives.

Encouraging a Thankful Mindset in Daily Life

In the quest to raise grateful and humble children in today's entitled world, one of the most crucial aspects is instilling a thankful mindset in their daily lives.

By fostering gratitude in children, parents can help them develop a positive outlook, empathy, and a sense of appreciation for the things they have.

Here are some strategies to encourage a thankful mindset in children:

Model Gratitude: Children learn by observing the behavior of their parents and caregivers. Therefore, it is essential for adults to model gratitude in their own daily lives. Expressing appreciation for the little things, saying thank you, and showing kindness to others can have a profound impact on children's attitudes towards gratitude.

Practice Daily Gratitude: Encourage children to reflect on their day and identify things they are thankful for.

This can be done through simple activities such as keeping a gratitude journal, where they write down one thing they are grateful for each day.

By regularly practicing gratitude, children can train their minds to focus on the positives in life.

Celebrate Small Victories: Acknowledge and celebrate even the smallest achievements or moments of joy in your child's life.

This could be as simple as praising them for helping out with chores, showing kindness to a friend, or achieving a personal goal.

By celebrating these small victories, children learn to appreciate their efforts and the positive impact they can have on others.

Encourage Acts of Kindness: Engaging in acts of kindness towards others can cultivate a sense of gratitude in children.

Encourage your child to perform random acts of kindness, such as helping a neighbor, volunteering at a local charity, or making a handmade card for a friend. By experiencing the joy of giving and making others happy, children can develop a deeper appreciation for the blessings in their own lives.

Teach Perspective-Taking: Help children understand that not everyone is as fortunate as they are. Expose them to different perspectives and experiences, such as volunteering at a soup kitchen or visiting a homeless shelter.

These experiences can help children develop empathy and a greater sense of gratitude for the privileges they have.

Express Appreciation: Encourage children to express gratitude towards others by saying thank you, writing thank you notes, or verbally acknowledging acts of kindness. By teaching children to show appreciation, they learn the value of gratitude in building positive relationships and fostering a sense of community.

Instilling gratitude from a young age can empower children to navigate the challenges of an entitled world with humility, appreciation, and a sense of abundance.

Fostering Humility

Exploring the Benefits of Humility in Children

Humility is a valuable trait that can have numerous positive impacts on a child's development and overall well-being.

In this section, we will delve into the benefits of humility in children and how cultivating this trait can have a lasting impact on their lives.

Enhanced Relationships

Humble children are more likely to have positive and meaningful relationships with others. They are empathetic, respectful, and considerate of other people's feelings and perspectives.

This can lead to stronger bonds with family members, friends, and peers, as well as better communication and conflict resolution skills.

Increased Empathy and Compassion

Humility allows children to recognize the humanity in others and develop empathy and compassion towards those around them.

By understanding and acknowledging their own limitations and imperfections, humble children are more likely to show kindness and understanding towards others who may be facing challenges or difficulties.

Improved Emotional Regulation

Humble children tend to have better emotional regulation skills, as they are more self-aware and able to manage their emotions in a healthy way.

They are less likely to react impulsively or defensively in difficult situations and are more open to feedback and constructive criticism.

A Growth Mindset

Humility fosters a growth mindset in children, encouraging them to embrace challenges, learn from failures, and continuously strive for self-improvement.

Humble children are more likely to be resilient in the face of setbacks and setbacks, as they understand that success is not solely based on innate talent but also on hard work and perseverance.

Gratitude and Appreciation:

Humble children are more likely to be grateful for the blessings in their lives and appreciate the efforts of others.

They understand the value of humility and are thankful for the support and opportunities they receive, leading to a greater sense of contentment and fulfillment.

Leadership Skills

Contrary to popular belief, humility is not a sign of weakness but rather a strength that can enhance leadership qualities in children. Humble leaders are able to listen to others, collaborate effectively, and inspire trust and respect among their peers. By cultivating humility, children can become effective leaders who prioritize the well-being of their team and work towards shared goals.

Overall, instilling humility in children can have a transformative effect on their character and behavior.

Emphasizing the importance of humility in the upbringing of children can enable parents and caregivers can help nurture a generation of individuals who are compassionate, resilient, and capable of making a positive impact on the world around them.

Ways to Nurture Humility in Children

Lead by example

Children learn a great deal by observing their parents and caregivers. Demonstrating humility in your own actions and words can set a powerful example for them to follow.

Show appreciation for others, admit when you make mistakes, and avoid boasting or seeking attention.

Encourage perspective-taking

Help children understand that everyone has their own strengths and weaknesses. Encourage them to consider other people's feelings and perspectives, and to practice empathy. This can help them develop a more humble approach to their own abilities and achievements.

Teach gratitude

Gratitude is closely linked to humility, as it involves recognizing and appreciating the contributions of others.

Encourage children to express thanks for the things they have, the help they receive, and the opportunities they are given. This can help them develop a sense of humility by acknowledging the role of others in their lives.

Foster a growth mindset

Encourage children to view challenges and setbacks as opportunities for growth and learning. Emphasize the importance of effort and perseverance, rather than focusing solely on outcomes or achievements.

By instilling a growth mindset, you can help children develop humility by valuing the process of learning and improvement.

Promote acts of service

Engaging children in acts of service and kindness towards others can help cultivate humility.

Encourage them to volunteer, help those in need, or contribute to their community in meaningful ways.

By experiencing the impact of their actions on others, children can develop a sense of humility and a greater appreciation for the interconnectedness of all people.

Encourage self-reflection

Encourage children to reflect on their own thoughts, feelings, and actions. Help them recognize their strengths and areas for growth, and guide them in setting realistic goals for self-improvement.

Fostering self-awareness and introspection can help children develop humility by acknowledging their own limitations and striving for personal growth.

Incorporating these strategies into your parenting or caregiving approach will enable you nurture humility in children and guide them towards becoming grateful and humble individuals in an entitled world.

Teaching Children the Value of Empathy and Perspective-Taking

Teaching children the value of empathy and perspective-taking is a crucial aspect of raising grateful and humble children in today's entitled world.

Empathy is the ability to understand and share the feelings of others, while perspective-taking involves seeing things from another person's point of view.

By nurturing these skills in children, parents can instill a sense of compassion, understanding, and humility that will serve them well throughout their lives.

Why Teach Empathy and Perspective-Taking?

Empathy and perspective-taking are essential for fostering positive social interactions, building strong relationships, and promoting a sense of community and connection with others.

Children who are able to empathize with others are more likely to display kindness, generosity, and consideration towards their peers.

Furthermore, developing these skills can help children navigate conflicts, resolve misunderstandings, and communicate effectively with others.

Strategies for Teaching Empathy and Perspective Taking

Model Empathy

Parents can lead by example by demonstrating empathy in their own interactions with others.

By showing compassion, understanding, and respect towards others, children can learn the value of empathy through observation.

Encourage Emotional Expression

Create a safe space for children to express their emotions and feelings. Encourage them to talk about how they are feeling and validate their emotions.

This helps children develop an awareness of their own emotions and can lead to a greater understanding of others' feelings.

Practice Active Listening

Teach children the importance of listening attentively to others without judgment. Encourage them to ask questions, show interest in others' experiences, and reflect back what they have heard to demonstrate understanding.

Engage in Perspective-Taking Activities

Encourage children to put themselves in someone else's shoes by engaging in perspective-taking activities. For example, you can ask them to imagine how a friend might feel in a certain situation or discuss different viewpoints on a particular topic.

Discuss Real-Life Scenarios

Use real-life examples to highlight the importance of empathy and perspective-taking.

Discuss news stories, books, or movies that showcase characters demonstrating empathy or facing challenges that require understanding others' perspectives.

Encourage Kindness and Helping Others

Emphasize the value of kindness, generosity, and helping others in building empathy. Encourage children to perform acts of kindness, such as sharing, helping a friend in need, or volunteering in the community.

Benefits of Teaching Empathy and Perspective-Taking

By teaching children the value of empathy and perspective-taking, parents can help them develop important social and emotional skills that will benefit them in various aspects of their lives.

Children who are empathetic and can take others' perspectives into account are more likely to form meaningful relationships, communicate effectively, and navigate social situations with grace and understanding.

Additionally, fostering empathy can help children become more grateful, humble, and appreciative of the world around them, leading to a more fulfilling and compassionate life.

Setting Boundaries and Limits

Establishing Clear Boundaries to Prevent Entitlement

Establishing clear boundaries is a crucial aspect of raising grateful and humble children in today's entitled world.

By setting and enforcing boundaries, parents can help their children understand the value of hard work, respect, and gratitude.

Here are some key strategies for establishing clear boundaries to prevent entitlement:

Communicate Expectations Clearly

It is essential to clearly communicate your expectations to your children regarding behavior, responsibilities, and privileges.

Explain the reasons behind the rules and boundaries you set so that your children understand the purpose and importance of following them.

Consistent Enforcement

Consistency is key when it comes to enforcing boundaries. Be firm and consistent in upholding the rules you have established.

This will help your children understand that there are consequences for their actions and that boundaries are non-negotiable.

Encourage Responsibility

Assign age-appropriate responsibilities to your children and hold them accountable for completing them.

Giving your children tasks to accomplish will help you teach them the importance of taking initiative, being responsible, and contributing to the family unit.

Limit Material Possessions

In today's consumer-driven society, children are often bombarded with messages that equate material possessions with happiness and success.

By setting limits on material possessions and teaching your children the value of experiences and relationships over things, you can help them develop a more grateful and humble outlook on life.

Promote Empathy and Generosity

Encourage your children to think about others and practice empathy and generosity.

Engage in activities that promote giving back to the community or helping those in need.

Instilling a sense of empathy and compassion in your children will enable you help them develop a more humble and grateful attitude towards life.

Model Humility

Children learn by example, so it is essential for parents to model humility and gratitude in their own behavior. Demonstrate acts of kindness, appreciation, and humility in your interactions with others. By showing your children how to be humble and grateful, you set a positive example for them to follow.

Encourage a Growth Mindset

Encourage your children to adopt a growth mindset, where they see challenges as opportunities for growth and learning.

Teach them that success is not always easy or immediate, and that hard work and perseverance are essential for achieving their goals.

By fostering a growth mindset, you help your children develop a sense of humility and gratitude for their own abilities and achievements.

It requires patience, consistency, and positive role modeling, but the rewards of cultivating these qualities in children are invaluable for their personal development and well-being.

Teaching Children the Concept of Delayed Gratification

Teaching children the concept of delayed gratification is a crucial aspect of raising grateful and humble children in today's entitled world.

Delayed gratification is the ability to resist the temptation of an immediate reward in order to receive a larger or more enduring reward later on.

This skill is essential for building resilience, self-discipline, and patience in children.

One effective way to teach children about delayed gratification is to provide them with opportunities to practice waiting for rewards.

For example, parents can set up scenarios where children have to wait for a treat or a special activity instead of receiving instant gratification.

This could involve tasks such as saving allowance money to buy a desired toy or waiting to open a special gift on their birthday.

It is important for parents to model delayed gratification themselves, as children learn best through observation and imitation.

Parents can demonstrate this concept by setting goals for themselves and working towards them patiently over time. By showing children how to delay their own gratification, parents can instill the value of hard work and perseverance.

Another helpful strategy is to engage children in discussions about the benefits of delayed gratification.

Parents can explain how waiting for a reward can lead to greater satisfaction and long-term success.

By helping children understand the concept of trade-offs and the importance of delayed gratification, parents can empower them to make wise choices and resist instant gratification.

In addition, parents can encourage children to set goals and create a plan to achieve them. By breaking down larger goals into smaller, manageable steps, children can learn the value of patience and persistence.

Celebrating small victories along the way can also reinforce the idea that delayed gratification is worth the effort.

Overall, teaching children the concept of delayed gratification is a valuable life skill that can help them develop resilience, self-discipline, and gratitude.

By providing opportunities to practice waiting for rewards, modeling patience and perseverance, engaging in discussions about the benefits of delayed gratification, and encouraging goal-setting, parents can empower their children to navigate the challenges of an entitled world with humility and gratitude.

Balancing Discipline and Positive Reinforcement

Balancing discipline and positive reinforcement is crucial when it comes to raising grateful and humble children in today's entitled world.

This balance involves setting clear expectations and boundaries while also recognizing and rewarding positive behavior. Here are some key points to consider:

Setting Clear Expectations

Discipline starts with setting clear expectations for your children. Clearly communicate what behaviors are acceptable and what are not. Be consistent in enforcing these rules so that your children understand what is expected of them.

Implementing Consequences

When rules are broken, it's important to implement consequences. However, discipline should be about teaching rather than punishing.

Consequences should be fair and related to the misbehavior. For example, if a child doesn't complete their chores, they might lose a privilege like screen time.

Using Positive Reinforcement

Positive reinforcement involves rewarding good behavior to encourage its repetition. This can be done through praise, encouragement, or rewards such as extra playtime or a small treat. Positive reinforcement helps children understand what behaviors are valued and appreciated.

Being Consistent

Consistency is key when balancing discipline and positive reinforcement.

Children need predictability to feel secure and understand the consequences of their actions. Inconsistency can lead to confusion and a lack of respect for rules.

Encouraging Self-Reflection

Help your children understand the reasons behind the rules and consequences. Encourage them to reflect on their behavior and how it impacts others. This can help cultivate empathy and a sense of responsibility.

Modeling Behavior

Children learn by example, so it's important to model the behavior you want to see in them. Show gratitude, humility, and respect in your own interactions with others. Your actions speak louder than words.

Open Communication

Keep the lines of communication open with your children.

Encourage them to express their feelings and concerns, and be willing to listen and discuss any issues that arise. This can help build trust and strengthen your relationship with them.

By finding the right balance between discipline and positive reinforcement, you can help your children develop a sense of gratitude and humility in a world that often promotes entitlement.

This approach fosters a healthy understanding of responsibility, respect, and empathy, laying the foundation for raising well-rounded and appreciative individuals.

Modeling Gratefulness and Humility

The Role of Parents as Role Models in Shaping Children's Attitudes

Parents play a crucial role in shaping their children's attitudes towards gratitude and humility.

Children look up to their parents as their first and most influential role models, observing and absorbing behaviors, values, and attitudes from them.

Lead by Example

Parents are the primary example that children observe and learn from on a daily basis.

Children are more likely to adopt attitudes and behaviors that they see modeled by their parents. Therefore, it is essential for parents to lead by example and demonstrate gratitude and humility in their own actions and interactions.

Whether it is expressing thanks, showing appreciation, or demonstrating humility in success and failure, parents' behaviors serve as a powerful model for their children to emulate.

Open Communication and Discussion

Parents can actively engage in open communication with their children about the importance of gratitude and humility.

By discussing real-life examples, sharing personal experiences, and highlighting the positive impact of these qualities, parents can help children understand the significance of cultivating these attitudes.

Encouraging children to express their feelings and thoughts about gratitude and humility also fosters a deeper understanding and appreciation for these values.

Creating a Gratitude Practice

Parents can create a culture of gratitude within the family by incorporating regular practices that promote appreciation and thankfulness.

This can include activities such as keeping a gratitude journal, expressing gratitude during family meals, or engaging in acts of kindness towards others.

By making gratitude a part of daily life, parents can instill in their children the habit of acknowledging and appreciating the blessings in their lives.

Parents can teach humility by emphasizing the importance of empathy and compassion towards others. Encouraging children to consider different perspectives, show kindness towards others, and practice humility in success and achievements helps cultivate a sense of humility and understanding of one's place in the world.

By demonstrating empathy and compassion in their own actions, parents can model humility and encourage children to do the same.

In conclusion, parents play a pivotal role in shaping their children's attitudes towards gratitude and humility.

By serving as positive role models, engaging in open communication, creating a culture of gratitude, and teaching humility through empathy and compassion, parents can help instill these essential qualities in their children and guide them towards becoming grateful and humble individuals in an entitled world.

Practicing Gratitude and Humility in Everyday Interactions

In today's fast-paced and materialistic society, it is more important than ever to instill values of gratitude and humility in our children.

By teaching them to appreciate what they have and to approach others with respect and modesty, we can help them navigate a world that often promotes entitlement and self-centeredness.

One of the key ways to cultivate gratitude and humility in children is through everyday interactions. These interactions provide countless opportunities for parents to model and reinforce these values in their children.

Here are some practical strategies for parents to incorporate into their daily routines:

Expressing Thankfulness

Encourage your children to express gratitude for the things they have, whether it's a meal on the table, a toy they received, or a kind gesture from a friend.

Teach them to say "thank you" and to acknowledge the efforts of others in their lives.

By making gratitude a habit in everyday interactions, children learn to appreciate the blessings around them.

Showing Appreciation

Help your children understand the value of hard work and kindness by praising their efforts and the efforts of others.

Whether it's a sibling who helped with a chore or a teacher who went the extra mile, point out these acts of kindness and generosity.

By highlighting the positive actions of others, you teach your children to appreciate the contributions of those around them.

Modeling Humility

Demonstrate humility in your own interactions by admitting when you make mistakes and showing appreciation for the help and support you receive. By modeling humility, you teach your children that it's okay to be imperfect and that everyone has room to grow and learn. Encourage them to approach challenges with a humble attitude, willing to listen and learn from others.

Practicing Generosity

Encourage your children to share their time, talents, and resources with others in need.

Whether it's volunteering at a local charity or helping a friend in need, teach them the joy of giving back to the community.

By practicing generosity in everyday interactions, children learn the value of selflessness and the importance of helping those less fortunate.

In conclusion, by emphasizing gratitude and humility in everyday interactions, parents can help their children develop a strong moral compass and a deep appreciation for the world around them.

These values will not only benefit them personally but also contribute to a more compassionate and harmonious society.

Through consistent modeling, encouragement, and reinforcement, parents can empower their children to navigate the challenges of an entitled world with grace and integrity.

Overcoming Challenges and Building Resilience

In the journey of raising grateful and humble children in today's entitled world, parents may encounter various obstacles that can hinder their efforts.

Understanding and addressing these obstacles is crucial to fostering a sense of gratitude and humility in children.

The following are some common obstacles and strategies to overcome them:

Materialism and Consumerism
One of the biggest challenges in raising grateful and humble children is the pervasive influence of materialism and

consumerism in society. Children are constantly bombarded with messages that equate happiness and success with material possessions. To counter this influence, parents can:

- Emphasize the value of experiences over material possessions.
- Encourage gratitude for what they have rather than focusing on what they lack.
- Teach children the importance of giving back to others and sharing their resources.

Instant Gratification

In today's fast-paced world, children are accustomed to instant gratification and may struggle with delayed gratification.

This can lead to a sense of entitlement and impatience. Parents can help children overcome this obstacle by:

- Teaching the importance of patience and perseverance in achieving goals.

- Encouraging children to work towards long-term rewards rather than seeking immediate satisfaction.

- Setting limits on instant gratification behaviors, such as excessive screen time or impulse buying.

Comparison and Social Media

With the rise of social media, children are constantly exposed to curated images of others' seemingly perfect lives, which can fuel feelings of inadequacy and envy.

To address this challenge, parents can:

- Foster a healthy self-esteem in children by emphasizing their unique strengths and qualities.

- Encourage open conversations about the

unrealistic nature of social media portrayals.
- Teach children to appreciate their own journey and accomplishments without comparing themselves to others.

Lack of Role Models
In some cases, children may lack positive role models who exemplify gratitude and humility. Parents can fill this gap by:
- Modeling gratitude and humility in their own words and actions.
- Exposing children to diverse role models from various backgrounds who demonstrate these values.
- Encouraging children to seek out mentors who embody the qualities of gratitude and humility.

By addressing these common obstacles in raising grateful and humble children, parents can create a nurturing environment that cultivates these essential values in their children, helping them navigate the challenges of an entitled world with grace and resilience.

Strategies for Navigating Peer Pressure and Societal Influences

Navigating peer pressure and societal influences is a crucial aspect of raising grateful and humble children in today's world.

The following are some strategies for parents to help their children resist peer pressure and societal influences

Open Communication

Encouraging open communication between parents and children is essential for tackling peer pressure. Parents can create a safe space for their children to share their experiences, concerns, and struggles without fear of judgment. By fostering a trusting relationship, parents can better understand their children's challenges and provide guidance accordingly.

Teaching Critical Thinking

Empowering children with critical thinking skills is a powerful tool against peer pressure.

Parents can help their children question and evaluate the influences around them, teaching them to think independently and make informed decisions.

By encouraging children to analyze situations critically, parents equip them with the ability to resist negative influences.

Setting Boundaries

Establishing clear boundaries and expectations is important in helping children navigate peer pressure.

By defining what is acceptable behavior and what is not, parents help their children make choices aligned with their values.

Setting boundaries also instills a sense of responsibility and self-discipline in children, making them less susceptible to external pressures.

Building Self-Esteem

Strengthening children's self-esteem is crucial for combating societal influences that promote materialism and superficiality. Parents can boost their children's confidence by highlighting their strengths, celebrating their achievements, and encouraging them to embrace their uniqueness. Children with a strong sense of self-worth are more likely to resist societal pressures to conform and seek validation from external sources.

Modeling Behavior

Parents play a significant role in shaping their children's attitudes and behaviors. By modeling humility, gratitude, and resilience in the face of challenges, parents set a positive example for their children to follow.

Demonstrating kindness, empathy, and integrity in everyday interactions teaches children the importance of staying true to their values even in the face of peer pressure.

Encouraging Empathy

Cultivating empathy in children can help them resist negative peer influences and make compassionate choices.

Parents can encourage their children to consider the feelings and perspectives of others, promoting understanding and kindness in their social interactions.

By fostering empathy, parents equip their children with the emotional intelligence to navigate peer pressure with compassion and integrity.

Incorporating these strategies into parenting practices can help raise children who are resilient, confident, and capable of resisting negative peer pressure and societal influences. By empowering children to stay true to their values and cultivate gratitude and humility, parents can guide them towards a path of authenticity and fulfillment in an entitled world.

Building Resilience in Children to Combat Entitlement Tendencies

Building resilience in children is a crucial aspect of raising grateful and humble individuals in today's entitled world.

Resilience enables children to navigate challenges, setbacks, and disappointments with grace and determination, rather than succumbing to feelings of entitlement or giving up easily.

Here are some practical strategies to help foster resilience in children:

Encourage problem-solving skills

Teach children how to identify problems, brainstorm solutions, and take action to address challenges independently. By empowering them to find solutions on their own, you are helping them develop a sense of agency and self-efficacy, which are essential components of resilience.

Promote a growth mindset

Encourage children to view failures and setbacks as opportunities for growth and learning, rather than as indicators of their worth or abilities.

Help them understand that mistakes are a natural part of the learning process and that perseverance and effort are key to achieving success.

Celebrate effort, not just outcomes

Focus on praising children for their hard work, determination, and resilience, rather than solely on their achievements or accomplishments.

By emphasizing the process rather than the end result, you are instilling in them a sense of intrinsic motivation and a willingness to persist in the face of challenges.

Teach coping strategies

Help children develop healthy coping mechanisms to deal with stress, anxiety, and disappointment.

Encourage them to practice mindfulness, deep breathing exercises, or other relaxation techniques to manage their emotions effectively. By equipping them with these tools, you are fostering their ability to bounce back from adversity and remain resilient.

Encourage autonomy and independence

Provide children with opportunities to make decisions, take risks, and learn from their experiences.

By allowing them to take on age-appropriate responsibilities and challenges, you are helping them develop confidence in their abilities and resilience in the face of obstacles.

Model resilience

As a parent or caregiver, it is essential to model resilience in your own behavior. Demonstrate perseverance, adaptability, and a positive attitude in the face of challenges, so that children can learn by example how to navigate adversity with resilience and grace.

By implementing these strategies and fostering resilience in children, you can help combat entitlement tendencies and raise grateful and humble individuals who are equipped to thrive in an entitled world.

Encouraging Ongoing Reflection and Growth in Parenting

Encouraging ongoing reflection and growth in parenting is a crucial aspect of raising grateful and humble children in an entitled world.

This process involves parents continuously evaluating their own beliefs, behaviors, and attitudes towards parenting, and being open to making changes and improvements along the way.

Here are some key points to consider in this regard:

Self-awareness: Parents should strive to cultivate self-awareness regarding their parenting style, values, and goals. Reflecting on their own upbringing, personal experiences, and cultural influences can help parents understand the underlying motivations behind their parenting choices.

Mindful parenting: Practicing mindfulness can help parents stay present in the moment, regulate their emotions, and respond to their children with empathy and compassion.

Mindful parenting involves being aware of one's thoughts and feelings without judgment, which can lead to more intentional and effective interactions with children.

Seeking feedback: Parents can benefit from seeking feedback from trusted sources, such as partners, friends, or parenting experts.

Constructive feedback can provide valuable insights into areas where parents may need to improve or adjust their approach.

Continual learning: Parenting is a journey of continual learning and growth. Parents should be open to exploring new parenting strategies, techniques, and resources that align with their values and goals for raising grateful and humble children.

Reflective practices: Engaging in reflective practices, such as journaling, meditation, or discussions with other parents, can help parents process their thoughts and feelings about their parenting experiences.

Reflective practices can also promote self-discovery and insight into areas of strength and areas for improvement.

In conclusion, encouraging ongoing reflection and growth in parenting is essential for raising grateful and humble children in an entitled world.

By fostering self-awareness, practicing mindful parenting, seeking feedback, pursuing continual learning, engaging in reflective practices, and modeling humility and gratitude, parents can create a nurturing and supportive environment that promotes the development of these important values in their children.

Emphasizing the Long-Term Benefits of Raising Grateful and Humble Children

Emphasizing the long-term benefits of raising grateful and humble children is crucial in shaping their character and ensuring their success in various aspects of life.

By instilling these values early on, parents can set their children on a path towards a fulfilling and meaningful life.

One of the key long-term benefits of raising grateful and humble children is the development of strong interpersonal relationships. Children who are grateful and humble are more likely to appreciate the efforts of others, express gratitude, and show empathy towards those around them.

These qualities not only help in building positive relationships with family and friends but also serve as a foundation for successful professional relationships in the future.

Furthermore, grateful and humble children tend to have a more positive outlook on life. They are able to find joy and contentment in simple things, which can lead to greater overall happiness and well-being.

This positive mindset can help them navigate challenges and setbacks with resilience and optimism, ultimately contributing to their mental and emotional health in the long run.

In addition, raising grateful and humble children can also lead to a greater sense of fulfillment and purpose.

When children learn to appreciate what they have and show humility in their achievements, they are more likely to find meaning in their actions and contributions to the world.

This sense of purpose can drive them to make a positive impact on society and strive towards personal growth and self-improvement.

Moreover, grateful and humble children are more likely to become responsible and compassionate individuals. They understand the importance of giving back to others, helping those in need, and being mindful of their impact on the world. These values can shape them into responsible citizens who contribute positively to their communities and society as a whole.

Overall, emphasizing the long-term benefits of raising grateful and humble children not only sets them up for personal success and happiness but also cultivates a generation of individuals who are compassionate, empathetic, and conscientious members of society.

By prioritizing these values in parenting, parents can help shape a brighter future for their children and the world around them.

Navigating Disappointments and Setbacks

Disappointments and setbacks are an inevitable part of life. Whether it's not getting the desired grade on a test, losing a game, or facing a canceled event they were looking forward to, children will encounter moments when things don't go their way.

How we help them navigate these experiences can profoundly shape their character, fostering resilience, gratitude, and humility.

Embrace the Moment

First things first, acknowledge your child's feelings. It's important for them to know that it's okay to feel upset, frustrated, or disappointed. Saying something like, "I can see you're really upset about not making the team," validates their emotions and shows empathy. This sets the stage for a supportive conversation, where they feel heard and understood.

Reflect on the Experience

Once the initial emotions have settled, encourage your child to reflect on the experience.

Ask open-ended questions like, "What do you think you could do differently next time?" or "What did you learn from this situation?"

This helps them shift focus from the disappointment itself to the lessons that can be gleaned from it.

Shift the Perspective

Guide your child in seeing setbacks as opportunities for growth. This is where cultivating a growth mindset comes in handy.

Remind them that everyone faces challenges and that these moments are stepping stones to future success.

Share stories of famous individuals who faced significant setbacks but went on to achieve great things. This can be incredibly motivating and reassuring for them.

Celebrate Effort, Not Just Outcomes

It's crucial to emphasize the value of effort and perseverance over the outcome. Praise your child for their hard work, dedication, and the courage to try, regardless of the result. This reinforces the idea that effort is what truly counts and that they have control over their actions, even if the outcome isn't always in their favor.

Foster a Supportive Environment

Create a family environment where mistakes and failures are seen as part of the learning process.

Celebrate when someone in the family overcomes a challenge, and support each other through difficult times.

Knowing they have a strong support system at home can help children face disappointments with more confidence and resilience.

Practice Patience and Compassion

Finally, be patient and compassionate. Children, especially younger ones, may struggle to see the silver lining immediately.

Give them time to process their emotions and gently guide them toward a more positive outlook.

Your consistent support and understanding will help them develop the emotional tools they need to handle setbacks gracefully.

Teaching the Value of Hard Work and Patience

In a world that often celebrates instant success and quick rewards, instilling the values of hard work and patience in children can be a game-changer.

These values not only set them up for long-term success but also help them develop a deeper sense of appreciation and resilience. Here's how you can nurture these important traits in your child.

Set Realistic Goals

Help your child set realistic, achievable goals. Whether it's a school project, learning a new skill, or saving up for something special, break down the goal into smaller, manageable steps. This teaches them the importance of persistence and the satisfaction that comes from gradually working toward something.

Celebrate Effort and Progress

While achieving the end goal is important, celebrating the effort and progress along the way is crucial.

Praise your child for their hard work, dedication, and the incremental improvements they make. This reinforces the idea that the journey and the effort are just as important as the destination.

Encourage a Growth Mindset

Promote a growth mindset by encouraging your child to see challenges as opportunities to learn and grow. Emphasize that skills and abilities can be developed through effort and perseverance. When they face setbacks, remind them that these are temporary and can be overcome with hard work and patience.

Provide Opportunities for Hard Work

Give your child opportunities to work hard and experience the fruits of their labor. This could be through household chores, school projects, or extracurricular activities.

When they complete tasks on their own, they gain a sense of accomplishment and understand the value of putting in the effort.

Teach Delayed Gratification

In our instant-gratification culture, teaching delayed gratification is essential. Help your child understand that some of the best rewards come from waiting and working for them. For instance, if they want a new toy or gadget, encourage them to save up their allowance or earn it through chores. This teaches them to appreciate and value what they have worked for.

Share Stories of Perseverance

Introduce your child to stories of individuals who achieved great things through hard work and patience.

Whether it's a famous athlete, scientist, or even someone from your own life, these stories can inspire and motivate your child to keep going, even when the going gets tough.

Practice Patience Together

Patience is a skill that can be developed with practice. Engage in activities that naturally require patience, such as gardening, cooking, or building a model.

These activities teach children that good things often take time and effort to come to fruition.

Handle Frustration Positively

When your child feels frustrated by a challenging task, acknowledge their feelings and encourage them to keep trying.

Help them break the task into smaller steps and tackle each one at a time. Show them that persistence in the face of frustration is part of the process of achieving something worthwhile.

Use Positive Reinforcement

Positive reinforcement can go a long way in teaching hard work and patience. When your child demonstrates these qualities, acknowledge and praise their efforts.

This positive feedback reinforces the behavior and encourages them to keep striving.

Be Patient with Their Progress

Remember that learning the value of hard work and patience is a journey, not a destination. Be patient with your child as they develop these traits.

Celebrate their small victories and provide support and encouragement during setbacks. Your patience will help them internalize these values more deeply.

These traits not only contribute to their personal success but also help them develop a deeper appreciation for the effort and time that go into achieving meaningful goals.

With your guidance and support, your child can learn to embrace hard work and patience as integral parts of their journey to becoming resilient and grateful individuals.

Addressing Peer Pressure and Comparisons

Raising kids in today's fast-paced, hyper-connected world is no small feat. Peer pressure and constant comparisons can make children feel inadequate or overly competitive.

But with a little guidance, you can help your child navigate these challenges with grace and confidence. Let's explore how.

Understanding Peer Pressure

Peer pressure is a powerful force. It's the influence that children feel from their friends and classmates to conform to certain behaviors, attitudes, or appearances. This pressure can be positive—encouraging kids to try new activities or work hard in school—or negative, leading to risky behaviors or feelings of inadequacy.

To combat negative peer pressure, it's crucial to foster a strong sense of self in your child. Help them understand their own values and beliefs so they can stand firm when external influences try to sway them.

Building a Strong Sense of Self

One of the best defenses against peer pressure is self-confidence. Here are a few ways to build this in your child:

Encourage Individuality: Celebrate what makes your child unique. Whether it's their sense of humor, artistic talent, or kindness, help them see these qualities as strengths.

Model Self-Confidence: Children often mimic the behavior of their parents. Show confidence in your decisions and values, and your child is likely to follow suit.

Open Communication: Keep the lines of communication open. Let your child know they can talk to you about anything without fear of judgment. This builds trust and gives them a safe space to discuss their feelings and experiences.

Navigating Comparisons

In a world of social media and constant connectivity, comparisons are inevitable. Kids might compare themselves to their peers based on looks, achievements, or social status. These comparisons can lead to feelings of envy or inferiority.

Here's how to help your child handle comparisons in a healthy way:

Focus on Effort, Not Outcomes: Teach your child to value effort over results. Praise them for their hard work and persistence rather than just their achievements. This helps them understand that success is a journey, not a destination.

Limit Social Media Exposure: Social media can amplify feelings of inadequacy. Set reasonable limits on screen time and encourage offline activities that your child enjoys and excels in.

Practice Gratitude: Gratitude can counteract the negative effects of comparisons. Encourage your child to keep a gratitude journal where they note down things they're thankful for. This shifts their focus from what they lack to what they have.

Practical Exercises

To put these concepts into practice, here are a few exercises you can try with your child:

Role-Playing: Create scenarios where your child might face peer pressure. Role-play these situations and discuss different ways they can respond. This helps them feel prepared and confident in real-life situations.

Gratitude Jar: Keep a jar where family members can drop in notes about things they're grateful for. Read them together weekly to foster a sense of appreciation and positivity.

Vision Board: Help your child create a vision board with their goals, dreams, and things they love about themselves. This visual representation can boost their self-esteem and remind them of their unique path.

Navigating peer pressure and comparisons is a continuous journey. By fostering self-confidence, encouraging open communication, and practicing gratitude, you can help your child develop the resilience they need to thrive in an entitled world.

Remember, every step you take towards nurturing these values is a step towards raising a grateful and humble individual. And that, my friend, is something truly worth celebrating.

Coping with Materialism in a Consumer-Driven World

In our consumer-driven world, it's easy for kids to get caught up in the allure of having the latest gadgets, trendy clothes, or newest toys.

Materialism can lead to a constant cycle of wanting more and never feeling satisfied.

But don't worry, there are ways to help your child find happiness beyond material possessions.

Let's explore how to tackle this challenge together.

Understanding Materialism

Materialism is the belief that owning and acquiring goods is essential for happiness and success.

Children are bombarded with messages from advertisements, social media, and even their peers that reinforce this idea.

It's crucial to understand that materialism isn't just about wanting things—it's about the deeper need for validation, acceptance, and self-worth that these things seem to promise.

Encouraging Mindful Consumption

One of the first steps in coping with materialism is to teach your child the value of mindful consumption. Here are a few strategies to get started:

Discuss Wants vs. Needs: Help your child differentiate between what they want and what they truly need. You can make this a fun and educational activity by going through their belongings and categorizing items together.

Set a Good Example: Children learn a lot from observing their parents. Show them that you value experiences and relationships over material possessions. Share stories about times when you chose experiences over things and how it made you feel.

Practice Gratitude: Regularly practice gratitude as a family. Encourage your child to express thankfulness for the non-material aspects of their life, such as family, friends, nature, and health.

Fostering Non-Material Sources of Happiness

Material possessions can never replace the joy that comes from meaningful experiences and relationships.

Here's how to help your child find happiness beyond material things:

Encourage Hobbies and Interests: Help your child discover and cultivate hobbies that they enjoy.

Whether it's playing a sport, painting, reading, or gardening, these activities provide fulfillment that goes beyond material satisfaction.

Promote Giving Back: Volunteering and helping others can be incredibly rewarding. Find opportunities for your child to give back to the community, whether it's through a local charity, community service project, or simple acts of kindness.

Create Memorable Experiences: Focus on creating memories rather than buying things. Plan family outings, game nights, or camping trips. These experiences are not only enjoyable but also help build stronger family bonds.

Managing Social Influences

Peer pressure and social media can intensify materialistic desires. Here's how to help your child manage these influences:

Limit Social Media Exposure: Social media often showcases an unrealistic and materialistic lifestyle. Set reasonable limits on screen time and encourage your child to engage in offline activities.

Teach Critical Thinking: Discuss advertisements and social media content critically. Help your child understand the intent behind these messages and the difference between real life and the curated images they see online.

Encourage Positive Friendships: Guide your child towards friends who share similar values and interests. Positive peer influences can reinforce the importance of non-materialistic pursuits.

Practical Exercises

To reinforce these concepts, try incorporating these practical exercises into your daily life:

Gratitude Journaling: Encourage your child to keep a gratitude journal where they write down three things they are grateful for each day. This shifts focus from what they lack to what they have.

Family Giving Project: Start a family project where you all decide on a cause to support.

This could be donating toys, raising money for charity, or volunteering time. It teaches the value of giving and helps shift focus from getting to giving.

Mindful Shopping: Involve your child in creating a shopping list and sticking to it. Discuss why each item is needed and avoid impulse buys. This practice helps them understand the importance of thoughtful consumption.

Final Thoughts

Coping with materialism in a consumer-driven world is an ongoing process.

By encouraging mindful consumption, fostering non-material sources of happiness, and managing social influences, you can help your child develop a healthy relationship with material possessions.

Remember, it's about finding balance and helping your child understand that true happiness comes from within, not from the things they own.

And in this journey, every small step towards gratitude and simplicity is a big step towards a more fulfilling life.

Helping Kids Navigate Social and Academic Pressures

Today's kids face a myriad of social and academic pressures that can feel overwhelming at times.

Balancing friendships, fitting in, excelling in school, and planning for the future can be a lot for them to handle.

As parents, you have a pivotal role in helping your child navigate these pressures with resilience and confidence. Let's explore some strategies together.

Understanding Social Pressures

Social pressures come from peers, social media, and the desire to fit in. Kids might feel the need to conform to certain behaviors, dress a certain way, or participate in activities just to be accepted.

To help your child navigate these pressures:

Foster Open Communication: Make it clear that your child can talk to you about anything. Listen without judgment and offer support and understanding.

Sometimes, just knowing they have someone to talk to can alleviate a lot of stress.

Encourage Authenticity: Help your child understand that it's okay to be themselves.

Emphasize the value of individuality and that true friends will appreciate them for who they are, not for what they have or how they look.

Role-Playing Scenarios: Practice responses to common social pressures through role-playing. This can build your child's confidence in saying no or standing up for themselves in uncomfortable situations.

Managing Academic Pressures

Academic success is important, but it shouldn't come at the cost of your child's well-being. Here's how to help your child manage academic pressures:

Set Realistic Expectations: Encourage your child to do their best, but avoid setting unrealistic expectations. Celebrate their efforts and progress rather than just their achievements.

Develop Healthy Study Habits: Help your child create a study schedule that includes breaks and leisure time. Teach them effective study techniques and the importance of a balanced approach to schoolwork.

Promote a Growth Mindset: Encourage your child to view challenges as opportunities to learn and grow. Praise their effort, persistence, and improvement, rather than focusing solely on grades.

Balancing Social and Academic Life

Finding a balance between social activities and academics is key to a healthy, happy life. Here's how to support your child in achieving this balance:

Time Management Skills: Teach your child to prioritize tasks and manage their time effectively. Tools like planners or digital calendars can help them keep track of assignments, extracurricular activities, and social events.

Encourage Extracurricular Activities: Participation in sports, clubs, or hobbies can provide a healthy outlet for stress and a chance to develop new skills. Just ensure these activities don't overwhelm their academic responsibilities.

Mindfulness and Relaxation: Introduce your child to mindfulness practices like meditation, deep breathing, or yoga. These can help reduce stress and improve focus, making it easier to balance various demands.

Practical Exercises

Incorporating practical exercises can help your child apply these strategies in their daily life:

Daily Check-Ins: Set aside time each day to check in with your child about their day. Ask open-ended questions about their social interactions and schoolwork. This can help you identify any emerging issues early.

Study Break Activities: Encourage short breaks during study sessions for activities like a quick walk, a fun game, or a creative project. These breaks can refresh their mind and improve productivity.

Positive Affirmations: Help your child develop a list of positive affirmations they can say to themselves when feeling stressed or pressured. Statements like "I am capable," "I am enough," and "I can handle this" can boost their confidence.

Helping your child navigate social and academic pressures is an ongoing process.

By fostering open communication, setting realistic expectations, and encouraging a balanced lifestyle, you can support your child in managing these challenges with resilience and confidence.

Remember, your presence and support make a world of difference. Together, you can help your child thrive both socially and academically, building a foundation for a happy and successful future.

Conclusion

As we reach the end of this journey together, I hope you've found practical strategies, insightful tips, and a renewed sense of confidence in nurturing gratitude and humility in your children.

Parenting in an entitled world is undeniably challenging, but it's also incredibly rewarding. By fostering these values, you're not just raising good kids—you're shaping kind, resilient, and empathetic individuals who will contribute positively to society.

Embrace the Journey

Remember, this process is not about perfection. There will be bumps along the way, moments of frustration, and times when you might question if you're doing it right. Embrace these moments as opportunities for growth—for both you and your child. Every effort you make towards instilling gratitude and humility, no matter how small, is a step in the right direction.

Celebrate the Small Wins

Celebrate the small wins. Notice when your child shows gratitude without prompting, or when they choose humility in a situation where pride might have been easier.

These moments are victories. They are signs that your efforts are taking root, even if the progress sometimes feels slow.

Stay Connected

Keep the lines of communication open with your children. Be their sounding board, their guide, and their cheerleader. Let them know that it's okay to struggle and that making mistakes is part of learning.

Your unwavering support and understanding will help them navigate the pressures of an entitled world with greater ease.

Lead by Example

Your actions speak louder than words. Model the behavior you wish to see in your children.

Show gratitude in your daily life, practice humility in your interactions, and approach challenges with a positive attitude. Your children are watching and learning from you every day.

Foster a Supportive Environment

Create a home environment that values kindness, empathy, and mutual respect.

Encourage open discussions about values and the importance of being grateful and humble.

Surround your family with positive influences and engage in activities that reinforce these values.

Look Forward with Hope

As you continue this journey, look forward with hope and optimism. The world may be filled with challenges, but it's also filled with opportunities for growth and connection. By raising grateful and humble children, you're contributing to a future that values compassion and understanding over materialism and entitlement.

Final Thoughts

In a world that often seems obsessed with more—more possessions, more achievements, more validation—choosing to nurture gratitude and humility in your children is a profound and impactful decision.

It's a commitment to raising individuals who appreciate what they have, who value others, and who understand that true happiness comes from within.